Bly's Dust

Bly's Dust

New and Collected Poems

Dorothy Ellis Barnett

ALAMO BAY PRESS

SEADRIFT•AUSTIN

Bly's Dust

Copyright © 2018 by Dorothy Ellis Barnett

All rights reserved.
No part of this book may be reproduced or utilized in any form or by any means, electronic or mechanical, including photocopying, recording or by any information storage and retrieval system without permission in writing.
Inquiries should be addressed to

ALAMO BAY PRESS
Lowell Mick White, Editor / Diane Wilson, Activist
Pamela Booton, Director
825 W. 11th Street, Suite 114
Austin, Texas 78701
pam@almobaypress.com
www.alamopress.com

Versions of some of these poems have appeared in the following anthologies: *New Texas, At the Riverside, P@RT, Jack Rabbit,* and various other small journals. I am eternally grateful to those publications.

Dorothy Barnett
Bly's Dust
 p   cm   photographs

1.   Poetry—Texas Author 2. Poetry—Inspirational Journey 3. American Poetry—Twenty-first century 4. Texas Literature—Poetry
I. Title II. Author III. Monograph
PN 6014 B48 2018   810.809764 Ba

ISBN: 978-1-943306-13-8

Dedication

To my family, who make me whole.

Contents

Foreword xi

-I-

Where You're From 1
Flip a Coin/Roll the Dice 2
100% Cotton 3
Brown-ice 6
Fool's Gold 7
Reading the Comics and Loose Change 8
Then 10
5th Grade Math 12
The Memory Comes of Water 13
Red 14
A Still Space Opens 15
Lost and Found 16
My Brown Hands 20
Chameleons Watched 21
Beside My Sleeping Husband 22
Taking a Chance 23
Minnows Pausing 24
"This brain is unremarkable." 26
Threads 27
This Happens 28
Zilker Park—Easter Midnight 30
Bly's Dust 31
Zen and the Bridge Table 32
Ants 33

-II-

The Blue Cape	37
San Francisco	38
Somebody's Darling	39
A Simple Man and the End of the World	40
A Rock Collector's Requiem	42
Spiders	43
Estate Sale	44
The Dead Man Watches the Bad Angels	45
Far and Near Lives	46
Adornment	47
Somewhere Around Willowbrook	48
Blizzards to Go	50
Redemption on the Drag	51
Andy Kaufman	52
In Lexa's Garden	53

-III-

I Wait for the Owl's Call	57
Circles of Power	59
Oaxaca	60
The Thirties	61
What Georgia O'Keefe Lost in Santa Fe, New Mexico	62
Afternoon Roads	63
Dreaming God	64

-IV-

Amendment 25	67
Flying into Baltimore	68
U.S. Invasion of Iraq	69
Near and Far	71
Now, what?	72
Girl Protection	73
"I touched their feet"	75

Canton, Texas	76
Sometime Sweetness	77
Escarpment	78
Cedar Fever	79
Spring	80
Broom-star	81
Enchanted Rock	83
Wild Things	85
Finding Texas	86
The Necessity of Empty Places	87

-V- Ansel Adams—Yosemite Photography

Spring/Water	91
Winter/Water	92
Winter/Air	93
Summer/Water	94
Spring/Air	95
Spring/Earth	96
Summer/Earth	97
Fall/Air	98
Fall/Earth	99
Summer/Air	100
Winter/Earth	101
Gratitude	103
About Dorothy Ellis Barnett	105
About the Cover Artist	107

Bly's Dust

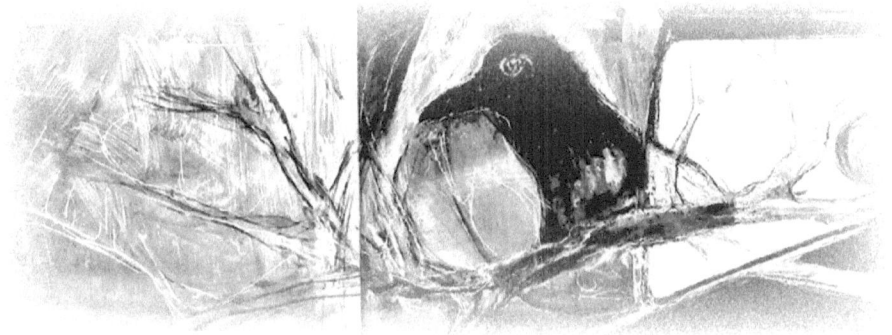

Foreward

IN THIS BOOK, I've included poems that reflect my life. I've always considered that poetry distills life into those moments that are important right then like photographs capturing an image. The energy created in the moment could be expressed in many ways. Joyce Carol Oats once said, "…poems can be paragraphs and paragraphs can be short stories and short stories can be novels." For now, these are the shortest versions of life's moments. I started writing poetry when I was told that there was too much poetry in my prose. I was young then and I would surely argue the point now. Many people are labeled by what they write; I've always tried to keep my options open by writing across genres. Imagine if you will that these poems may be waiting to become notes of longer pieces; I hope you enjoy them.

I

Where You're From

If you live long
enough in one place,
you'll learn the lay of the land:
know how far it is
to the Henly cut off,
that the best pie for miles
can be bought at the bowling
alley in Blanco, know the woman
called Grace who stood in her frontyard
and watched as her only daughter
was killed crossing the highway,
remember the red everywhere,
you'll know that the pinpoints of light
in the dark hills across the valley
belong to the Miller place,
know where your friend Marla
wanted to live one summer
several boyfriends ago,
know the trickle of the Comal,
the Blanco, the Pedernales,
the Guadalupe,
wet mantras that measure
how far you've been, you'll know
which stars guide you home.

Flip a Coin/Roll the Dice

How easy it has always been to think/wish myself away from my childhood. Easy to think that someone else could have adopted me, and my life would have been different/better. My life could have been decided by flipping a coin. Heads I go to live with Laura and Kenneth, tails I'm sent along another path. Recently my oldest daughter found Mary and Frank—Laura and Kenneth's friends at the time of my adoption. After telling me that Frank had taken his own life right in front of her—shot himself with a shotgun—gore ever where, Mary's voice over the phone became the raspy voice of too many cigarettes and too much whisky as she said, "I almost took you, but Kenneth and Laura wanted a baby, so I let them have you." Flip a coin/roll the dice, how simple.

100% Cotton

I.
We were travelers those years
riding the winding blacktop,
always reaching westward towards
the next river and back again
Row after row of heavy brown
plants, curled
and straight, clicked-
by, outside the car window
For miles the cotton fields released
white into drifts gathering in eddies
along the railroad tracks
New England snow-white
littered the Panhandle roadside
in dead of summer hell
At the roadside turnaround
we stopped for our lunch
of yellow-orange cheese
and big wheel bologna
sandwiches
In the distance I could see
the u-shaped stooped backs
of the pickers as they worked
their way down the long
rows stretching out
a lifetime

My mother's hand took me
into the fields to touch the white
bolls of her history, we waded past

knife sharp brown leaves waist
high, we waded deep into the field,
our car a faded blue speck
under the trees in the distance
My mother's hand took mine there
in the field, she covered the boll
with our hands, her hand, my hand
the soft white hidden by brown broken
sharp as glass blades

II.
My mother's people came
from Oklahoma dirt to Texas
during the Depression
Her mother walked barefoot on the reservation,
twisted her long black hair into a braided
crown, dipped brown acrid snuff
and married a Dutchman wandering through
They worked the hard land for
fourteen years and thirteen babies
before the dust nearly buried them
then they let the dry wind blow
them south to Houston
Where tent city slums waited and poverty
wore the color gray, where muddy
water gathered around the base
of communal copper spigots, where
mosquitoes and dusty shell roads
stretched out a lifetime
My mother's father pulled her out

of school in the third grade, put her
in fields to pick cotton, to help out,
she was eight, years later he would crawl
into her bed at night, sink into her and
her cotton mattress, touch her while her mother cried
The fields of cotton-white clouds sweeping
the earth-became her haven,
her quick hands found the sticky
bolls fast and sure, she pulled her weight
fifty pounds, then a hundred, the long
full bag following behind in the narrow row,
stretching out her lifetime
The plants towered above her, hiding her,
her shape hiding, hiding her from his shape,
at thirteen she ran away, married a drunk
wandering through,
he kept her in the fields to help out,
years of abuse left the dry landscape
of her body barren

III.
That day of my childhood field, as our hands curled
around the cotton white, my mother's voice said,
there's a softness in life and a hardness
sometimes there's no difference
in the two
That day in the field-white, my mother's voice,
my mother's hand, my hand, the cotton,
sometimes all we have
are the memories.

Brown-ice

By the roadside gas station
in wintering Texas,
smooth bottles of semi-frozen
coke dropped kerchunk
through the silver chute
of the red machine
Frost on the car windows, frost on
on the ground, frost on the bottle,
frost on my breath leaving
spiraling out, waiting
for my father's knife to punch
open the top, its razor point
sure in his hand
His voice rushed over
the truck sounds speeding
"quick, catch it before
it spills," as the brown-coke
floe pushed up through the slender glass neck
This morning frost spreads hard
diamonds in the yard, binds
grass to moisture, the moon
sinks its crescent in the west
This morning walk sends
my breath out in white spirals
following the moon, I watch
them, wanting the taste of coke,
waiting my father's voice

Dorothy Ellis Barnett

Fool's Gold

Out of the back window of the car,
I see where I've been, see the landscape rushing away,
like old photos—black and white reminders of lives:
myself at eight standing in Colorado snow,
a white-flocked organza Christmas dress,
skirt too short above my knobby knees, hair
a wild tangle of black untamed curls
haloed around my face—fist by my side,
tight around a clump of just bought pyrite; false
like the love from your mouth,
I can still feel the cold metallic taste of it,
and across the snow my father's lengthening shadow
as he held the old black box camera.

Reading the Comics
and Loose Change

In the sultry afternoons
of Houston, side by side
on the sofa we'd sit,
my voice rising and falling
to the action on the paper page.
"Read another," he'd say
with his slurred voice.
"Read the one about Jughead
and Archie. I like that one.
Go on, Sister, read it
for your Uncle Floyd."
My Uncle Floyd couldn't read,
not a word, could barely
sign his name.
The last of my grandma's
fourteen kids, he was
the baby she held close
to her breast the longest.
I remember the boozy smell of him,
the way his skin seeped whisky,
the loose change he'd have
for ice cream....and I remember
my grandma as she rocked back
and forth in her lime green chair.
He was our secret, delicate,
the one that needed to be helped
the most, and shielded there
beneath the overhanging pines
and magnolias, we watched
as he pulled himself down

Dorothy Ellis Barnett

into the amber liquid.
I'd turn the pages and read to him
about Jughead, Archie, and Betty
sometimes making it up as I went
along. Over and over the same stories
floated out to cover the afternoon shadows.

Then

We were nine. I was small and skinny-thin
and too smart. Dora was six days
older and slow, already taller
than I would ever be, her breasts
trying to poke through the layers
of baby fat she'd never lose,
strong hands large and pale
one covered my two—which she liked,
squeezing them white-hard until I yelled
uncle.
My sin was reading
and knowing what the words meant
not just sounding them out
like she did, each syllable long
and slow—each sentence patched
together like a drunkard's path,
my voice was full and even, loud
so the grown-ups could hear. "Isn't that nice,
what a sweet child she is for helping Dora
with her reading."
Back then, while the grown-ups
played cards, the cousins gathered
in the bare side yard to tilt and joust;
each inch of turf carefully marked.
Dora lagged behind, the last one
picked, always. One day in a game
of follow, hand over hand we inched
along the wooden fence, feet dangling high
above the packed sand, Dora trailed.
The two meanest of us finished

Dorothy Ellis Barnett

first and ran victory-flushed to the back
of the line. They stood there taunting,

pushing her to go faster. I finished next,
stood back and watched as she cried;
they could turn so. The biggest
of us grabbed her legs, and she hung
on—her strong hands biting
into the rough wood—her mouth wide
open red. I stood back, watched
not joining, not helping—they could
turn so.
I remember the sound
of the back door screen and someone
rapping loudly on the glass window
before we scattered through the brittle
leaves, but I don't remember seeing her
let go.   Just as I don't remember how
hard it was to get up early to catch the school bus,
or trying to be good,
and I don't care about the remembering.
Just as I don't care about the cousin in Houston
who's a finisher now or the one driving silver rigs
outside of Lubbock, but I want to know
about Dora and what she did with the hurt
that afternoon in the side yard
of the house on South Main.

5th Grade Math

Long division was a mystery of symbols, but reading skills had sorted her into the fifth grade where numbers and rules for numbers lived and breathed. To think that six went into eighteen was an agreeable thing, but two into five caused problems. No one seemed interested that she thought remainders meant there were leftovers of sum sort and then there was that curious incident with the pi, where the leftovers never ended, that sent her mind spiraling searching for infinity.

The Memory Comes of Water

I was so little, no more than six
or so. We were in the shower,
my mother washing my hair—I remember:
the green stinging soap in my eyes-her insistence
that I be still, keep my head back, water
cascading over my face—wet—smothering.
My struggles became louder, my lungs searched
for air—still she kept my head back.

I've never thought to question
the image. My father's hands reaching
through, pulling me to safety, past
our reflections on the cold, wet
white tiles, her blank stare,
the plastic shower curtain torn
from its metal rings, one red corner
still caught by the rod, he wrapped
me in a rough-white towel, carried
me out to sit in the sun—light.

Later, when I should have been asleep,
his voice low-hard from their bedroom.
"*If you ever touch her again, I'll kill you.*"
So, she didn't.

I never thought to question the image
until someone said, "*Tell me when
you stopped being
your mother's daughter.*"

Red

The woman in the red dress
looks in the mirror and thinks
about the color red:
wonders when it became
a bad color, thinks about scarlet
and Hester's letter,
thinks about blood red, wonders why
monthly bleeding is a curse,
thinks about red light districts,

Wonders about berries pyracantha,
nandana, holly and yupon, wonders
about the colors crimson, carmine,
cerise,

Thinks about the red cracks
in the mahjong tiles, written prayers
on red paper left twisting in the wind,
remembers cardinals flying red
through the wintering trees,

The woman wearing the color red
wonders about her Aunt Ruby,
she looks in the mirror and
remembers red was her mother's
favorite color—remembers her
red lipstick stains on wine glasses—
remembers
not wearing red for thirty years.

Dorothy Ellis Barnett

A Still Space Opens

or Why I Paid a Hundred Dollars for a Brick
with My Mother's Name on It

Sometimes in my just waking mind
a door will open—then close
and I hold my breath

The gentle sound of my husband's steps
becomes my father's heavy tread
and I hold my breath, wait

for my mother's voice
sounding soft, counterpoint
to my father's shouting

Sometimes in my just awake body
a still space opens that shows me how
far I've come, how far yet to go

Lost and Found

I. Birth
My mother must have held me
before I was born, rocked me,
cradled me in moonlight.
Maybe she wrapped her strong arms
around her ripe belly and sang
a lullaby before letting go.

I must have floated in love
like a small brown skiff.
They say we know these things:
maternal pulse sure as sudden red,
the shadowed voice, the primal smells
that call us home.

If I saw *her* again, could place
my head against the hollow between
the swell of *her* breasts would
it be like *my* baby's laugh
as known as *her* smell.

II. Adoption
Turn the dark pages
white before words,
see the one called
mother and remember.

See the small chin tightly held,
green washcloth rubbed too hard,
wooden hairbrush
pulled through tangles,

Dorothy Ellis Barnett

see the silence cover the room
see the father become the mother
see the silence covering the house.

Our lives are rooted in these words:
love, your mother, always.
We say them, they mean
nothing, they mean everything.

III. Jeana
She was someone else's mother
but belonged to me. My life happens
now without her. I turn to hear
her voice when she's not there.
I put her cloak on, take
her brushes in my hand, sweep
her colors across my canvas.

IV. My daughters—Laura and Cory
Both my daughters tell this story:
"*in the afternoons, when we were little
you would take us to your
big bed and say you look sleepy,
you need a nap, then your eyes
would slowly close.
We would sit there for a while
like cautious cats then slide away
over the edge, to let you sleep.*"

These two did not slip easily

from my body. They pressed
against me, their hot fragrance
spilling heavy. Even then I held
to them, not wanting the division
of waters and breath, afraid
of the loss.

V. Reagan
Baby boy sweet
boy baby, our baby,
you floated in love
a small skiff nestled safe
snug in your mother's harbor
waiting to be found
your hair a wet, dark cap
your tawny petaled skin glistening
in mother's liquid-love
your first gasping breath
a heralding cry
we heard your voice
loud, strong
sangre mio
sangre mio
our lives happen
now with you

VI. Hudson
You joined our tribe
our Nordic wonder;

where did you come
from with your flaxen
hair and stout soldier
trudging steps?

Only two and yet you
command the troops,
as you march behind
your big brother.

Only your sable brown eyes
are familiar, are what's
left of the journey.

VII. Paige
There you were—waiting
to join us so we could be
complete—your blood our
blood, your dance our dance,
your song our song—stronger
now because of you.

My Brown Hands

are short and in 4 a.m. morning stillness
hold crying babies and men. They pound on oak
tables in anger, and pound
out dough for steaming ovens—browned
bread their siren's song.

Shaped oval-smooth and shiny,
the nails no longer clog
with rough grog they've pulled
to the wet surface of a potter's wheel.

Only the middle right finger,
that used to wave in protest,
now aches in the morning cold
or crows when the weather changes,
and (so I've been told) they all wear too much
silver and turquoise
to sing Bach.

Chameleons Watched

Last night, I watched my sleeping self,
curled, knees to chest,
grandmother's wedding quilt
tight around me like a shroud.

On a tall ficus tree rooted
beside my bed, small, smooth chameleons
perched at each bare branch tip,
hundreds of them—brown to green
green to brown—weighing the slender branches
down until they dripped like willow.

Last night, as I lay sleeping
still chameleons watched. I stirred to wake;
they flocked wing to wing, a swooping flight
of snow geese on a Montana plain,

escaping out the open window,
into the crystal night.

Beside My Sleeping Husband

Sometimes at night when I lie awake
beside my sleeping husband, his touch still warm
against my skin, I can see through the window,
out past Lady Bank's rose, stars shining like hot diamonds.

Luciferous flecks, brilliance dead before last glimmer,
some still dying. Once, there in the corner of light,
where the moonspider casts down its web of gold,
one lost its delicate footing and fell,
straight through the sky it seemed,
a certain urgency to its journey.

Would someone wear widow's weeds for this lone voyage
of fading luminescence. Would someone know
its falling fate. I turn to cup against my mate's naked back
and hope he knows that I am here.

Taking a Chance

The spring I was seventeen, Bryon Tunnell Day in Tyler, Texas, 1963 was celebrated in the Rose Garden on the county fairgrounds. I can't remember why Mr. Tunnell needed a celebration, but someone thought he did, but that's not important. Who was Bryon Tunnell? Texas Railroad Commissioner – but that's not important. What is important is that Francis Fix and a friend whose name has been lost to me, invited me to go on a blind date with an "older" student who attended TJC (Tyler Junior College). What is important is that I had never been on a blind date before, had only been on three other dates if you discount going to the movies with the gypsy boy when I was eight or nine. What is important is that on the night Bryon Tunnell was celebrated among thousands of roses blooming in every color, their scent hanging heavy in the air, I met my husband on a blind date. Someone asked me recently if I thought he had saved me – yes, he did and I saved him. We are still saving each other fifty years later.

Minnows Pausing

one by one her friends
need bifocals, cultivate personal physicians
over the bridge table, they joke about Depends,
going to the kitchen, forgetting the why
and not remembering names

twice, she's forgotten how to turn
on the dryer
the first time, her husband
a practical man, said, *push the button*
what button she asked from the depths
of the laundry room
the second time, he wasn't there

dry hands and mouth, thundering flashes of heat,
and trace chemicals her body needs
but no longer makes
pills—pink, blue, yellow
pale baby colors for the bloodless womb

the grown children warn
that she's in the fast-lane going slow,
want to know why she keeps a bottle
of water and food in the car

her friends dye their hair, have their chins
lifted, take trips now
while they can

she recalls an old love

that almost happened, remembers
the feel of his body floating close
to hers in the cold, clear river,
 wanting to be that water on his skin, remembers
the searing, summer warmth of flat rocks,
minnows pausing in dappled shadows

and now, she's in the middle
where there's a strange comfort in all these things
like the beacon on a far shore
she approaches across a tattered sea

"This brain is unremarkable."

(MRI lab report in February–2006)

The unremarkable brain lives in a world of words, where clean white margins surround student writing. Clean margins surround the lump in the breast of the body housing the unremarkable brain.

Sewing machine sounds invade the breast of the body, but the unremarkable brain does not think about the sounds; it thinks of cells—red, white, and others that are faster moving.

The word lump changes the meaning of sweetness, hair, as the unremarkable brain wonders about the female-erotic, wonders how much has really changed.

Rejecting the words *reoccurring* and *spreading*, the unremarkable brain does not think about the future, the past, thinks instead about a woman in Germany who injects mistletoe juice each day.

The unremarkable brain does not like the word survive—prefers conquer, prefers living in a land where bridges are blown up and armies do not advance across borders, and wonders if Rachael Carson felt alone in her silence, wonders if her garden was slashed, poisoned, and burned.

The unremarkable brain wakes in the full moon stillness of two a.m., knows more than it wants to know, watches as the word *promise* floats in the air. The unremarkable brain grabs it and holds on.

Threads

Water seeks lower ground when dirt gives way,
cells reach out to other cells,
come together then pull apart,
something appears where there was nothing,
pockets are turned inside out,
lives upside down,
what has to be is so quickly forgotten,
the sun sets and there is an empty moon,
even dreams hold dark silence, and
there is only one set of footprints leading away,
how quickly we unravel.

This Happens

I.
two men, boys really
are forced into a dark
car trunk—the car is let go
into the muddied flooded waters
of our town's lake

mothers cry—fathers
cry—our town cries
children are killing
each other

II.
a friend dies, chemo,
radiation and pills
have stretched his pale-white
skin taut, his daughter's
shadowy form passes
by death's doorway

in her face, your mind's eye
sees his old face—the one before,
you wonder about his death
poem—his regrets—you regret
missed visits, fishing lessons
lost, poems not shared

III.
on the driving range
while your husband reaches
for the perfect arc of arms, club

Dorothy Ellis Barnett

swing, white ball bounding
across the greens

you see an old friend's
husband—"*how's Nina,*"
you ask, "*haven't seen her
in ages*"

"*things change,*" he says, "*many
things change, we're not to-
gether anymore*"

"*but, we're trying to get on
with our lives, I'm taking up
golf, she's doing
other
things*"

IV.
you think about the words
reason cause sense random
and *chaos*—a law of nature,
you think about conflict—as part
of the ebb—flow
as natural as things going back
to normal

you think about books
of brittle paper—best
be careful how you turn
the pages

Bly's Dust

Zilker Park
Easter Midnight

Sometimes there is a stillness in the park and the empty swings seem unfamiliar. It is like that tonight. A lone yellow dog crosses the soccer field, stops its canter long enough to look back at my moon-silvered car. The dog and I move through this emptiness towards something else. He seems so sure of his destination. I know only the certainty of the next corner and the right turn into the neighborhood where I've lived for sixteen years. All those years, and yet, in this night quiet I feel that I don't belong among these native stone and red brick houses with pampered lawns. I remember the slat-backed familiarity of the wooden rocker on my grandmother's front porch, and long for the red sandy loam yard, the fireflies light across the road in the darkness of the hog wallow where they said Slick Brown disappeared. There is little history in my life now, a few black and white photos of giant sequoia, Oregon logging camps and faces fading from my memory. My children will remember other things and long for those. The cedar chest by my bed holds baby clothes from thirty years ago and little else.

Bly's Dust

for Robert Bly

The early morning sun sinks down
to fill my spirit-well.

My thoughts come close,
recede like snow
drifts against the house.

Through the window the old hackberry's
budshells curl around new yellow-
green potential

that will brood at the foot
of plants. I have slept
the night.

I will be like that
to last forever.

Zen and the Bridge Table

I made simple blunders at the bridge table yesterday—blunders that I knew not to make and as usual could not figure out why. This morning brought more clarity—the answer is Zen. There was no Zen for me yesterday since I was too caught up in the left-brain quantitative bidding process, which is far removed from the right-brain intuitive bidding. There was no watching each card, each play while blocking out the other players. I was not lost in the cards. Bridge has brought a curious tug of war between the creative self and the thinking self. Thinking, doing bridge is hard for me—being bridge, being the cards fits me better.

Ants

Each morning before sunrise
while the air is still waking
I make the coffee.

Each morning when I pour cold
fresh water into the reservoir
small ants float to the top.

Their small black bodies drift
in swirling eddies as
I dip them out with a silver-
handled strainer.

Some ants clutch to each other
with their fat pontoon bodies
making rafts, building bridges of brown
and red, so their kin can cross
to the other side.

My ants do not cling to brothers
and sisters or try to save themselves
but instead seem to give up as if they
welcomed the wash of water
pulling them under.

No raft builders these coffee ants,
no reaching out for help—My mother-in-law
died last week; given three months to live,
she died in one, far from home,

far from the East Texas piney woods
she loved, far from the place she wanted
her ashes—This morning as I made coffee
I thought of her.

II

The Blue Cape

for Jeana

Sometimes I wear it around
my shoulders like your shroud.
I've taken it as my own, put it on
like your skin, your white over my dark.
The fabric seems to still hold your shape
as if your breath had not yet escaped.

I would have written that last day
differently, shaped it into something other
than your pale form wrapped
in the rough green-cloth of strangers.

It should have come for you
from some white mountain, down
through the clouds to lift across the winds
to a waiting sea, the blue
cape trailing behind.

I will be years gathering
up what you've left to me, culling
through the paintings, searching
pockets for the staining
tints left by your brush.

And always the blue cape
will fold soft against my back,
the long hem licking at the ground,
old green paint from your palette coating
the fading threads, in the right pocket
a sable brush, waiting for your hand.

San Francisco

I wish that I was there
with you,
could wake to your day
could walk the up down streets
and stand on earth's edge
where great spans of rusted steel
connect, and watch waves of ships tugged out
to sea and see fine spun mist spread
over Muir's Woods deep
within a valley that rises up
where coral heather bows to sky
and the road leads down
to rocky sand,
to your footsteps
that walked away.

Dorothy Ellis Barnett

Somebody's Darling

South of town on Ben McCulloch Road
Somebody's darling straightened a curve,
left the blacktop,
met an oak head on.

A weathered note, faded
flowers, and a fuchsiaed cross
fixed the spot.

I stood on the very place
where *Somebody's* darling let go,
wished I could reach out and catch
the warmth, pull it back from the cold,

closer to home,
for *Somebody*.

A Simple Man
and the End of the World

A simple man hangs his medals against walls
that corner the brick fireplace, while outside
his wife tends the tall purple iris,
cedar wax wings descend to eat the wet
pyracantha berries hanging in red clusters,
and happy children splash
through puddles left by the rain
not knowing what falls away
is for always.

In the dojo, a simple man stills his heart,
between beats waits for the open
space of the Shodan warrior,
as he steps into the body of the master,
he is not afraid.
The white blind dog tastes the air

for the smell of the simple man,
waits for the sound of his voice.
Tables are sorrowed with the weight
of cakes and pies, tuna sandwiches
and stuffed celery.

No one believes it is happening now,
flowers are still beautiful,
blue skies hold still white clouds
students stroll across the campus
so many books wait to be read.
In a room full of strangers, the wife
of the simple man shakes the hand
of a woman she doesn't know and

says, "*I will miss him so much,*"
as she sees the end of the world.

A Rock Collector's Requiem

for B.A.

Sudden, like the smell of cinnamon,
he left one autumn day when blood
rushed to a place
it shouldn't be.

She found him, face pressed
against his polished stone
garden. I heard the tumbler turning,

sluicing for days, then someone
remembered to switch it off.
I watch her sometimes

my life facing hers,
across the cedar fence.
I see the stoop of her

shoulders as she reads
in fading shadows, opens
the door at dusk
to the deaf gray cat,

throwing yellow light
against the approaching dark.

Dorothy Ellis Barnett

Spiders

Like the two sister spiders
that sit on either side
of the dining room window,
the cells waited
and wove their web
to cast out
and grab the things inside
that were breaking down
and building up

and he didn't know, but
just withdrew for reasons
of his own. *"He's just old"*
they said, *"well over eighty
so of course, he's tired
and quiet. You would be too"*
they said.

So, they got him out of bed
in the morning, dressed him in flannel
to sit in the sun
as if that would help, would
keep the spiders from spinning
their fine threads of angel hair
over and around the things inside
that were breaking down
and building up.

Estate Sale

In the cold front room, we stand
at the foot of the bed,
the smooth white counterpane
our table, where only days before
her stilled heart was covered.

Her life is priced
with white stickers, "*Too cheap*,"
we say to a red-shirted man offering
loose change for the silver comb
she used each morning.

We close the blinds and doors and carry away
what doesn't sell: the plaster plaque
with your small hand print, her faded
green garden hat, photos of relatives
we don't know and four bent coat hangers.

We hold hands, down the steps
like before when we didn't need to
and at the bottom, I stop to water the river fern;
its brown fronds curl against the feet of roses
climbing purple against the voiceless walls.

Dorothy Ellis Barnett

The Dead Man Watches the Bad Angels

Live as if you were already dead, or about to die.

For Marvin Bell

When the dead man watches the bad angels in the communal bath,
    voyeurism is not his intent, the smell of soap and steam
    closing-in to cloud the room.
In the communal bath, the bad angels do not see the liquid dead man's
    rivulets running down the tile walls.
The dead man uses his words – stick, fizz, bone, bell, but none of them work.
The bad angels are too wet and sleepy, wanting only to ladle up the hearts of
    their brethren into their pockets, using pins, cotton, and
a pair of silk hammers.
By the flickering fluorescent lighting, they were too busy to listen.
The bad angels were instruments of balance wanting only a resemblance
    of Marvin's poems, but their words were weightless in
      comparison.
They had stayed up too late, could not see, nor hear the dead man.
The dead man thinks that *fog is a mirror* and the bad angels were never nuns.

Far and Near Lives

I wonder about those men
who ride the trains
swaying to and fro,
a sea legged gait
stumbling them
along the rails.

Do you think they see
the blackberry vines
bursting white against
the clacking track,
cherries turning deep red-wine,
and the old woman with greying
daughter who stops to wave us on
as our worlds slip quickly by?

Is it possible that they see
the ties of wood and metal
sweat spiked down
side by side years ago
by so many foreign hands?

Do they see the bodies
left where they fell,
bones turning to brittle mileage
markers no one reads?

Dorothy Ellis Barnett

Adornment

Young women, almost girls, wear their colors
dripping down their firm arms, entwining brillance
of reds, greens and blues.

Color reaches into the folds of their soft blouses
drips hidden onto their breasts
slides down their bared backs.

Vines reach encircling their necks, embracing
skin with green poppy leaves, yellow lotus blossoms,
and celtic symbols.

The patterns are often unfinished and wait for an artist's
hand to fill—
in between the lines, elaborate stories
waiting to be told in color.

My adornment is different, childbirth painted red lines
on my body, across my breasts and stomach, changing the
    contours.
Sometimes I wonder what stories my body could tell
if the lines were colored in artist's ink.

Somewhere Around Willowbrook

For Susan Vasquez

We never thought of what we were doing:
at fourteen we made up our own rules and went
to Saturday night dances with boys in cars,
Harbor Lights saxed low and tight skirts
of yellow, blue, silver and black swirled
around the dim dance floor.

I remember the red dress you let me borrow;
all afternoon we took it in, made it
tighter so it would hug my young curves
and cup my breasts. Straight skirts, high heels,
hair teased out to there, we were hot.

So many nights I spent at your house,
four rooms, one bath and six kids. Sleep
overs meant Jose moved up to the top
bunk so I could have the bottom space.
We were so sure of everything and knew
only the moment; you dreamed of college,

studied all the time to make straight A's,
to make it possible; I never studied
but kept up with you. You hated me for that
while I hated you for: your four-room house,
chicken mole simmering on the kitchen stove, fresh
tamales, turquoise parakeets screeching on the back porch,
your mother at the table always
holding a baby, and the father who didn't touch you.

Each week we changed the rules: this one could dance
with us, that one couldn't, no fast dances
only slow or we'd only dance when the cute guy
played a sax solo. The boys postured around anyway
waiting for something, none of us knew what but
thought we did.

Then the long ride home from East L.A. back
to Compton through the dark quiet streets,
the gentle swaying of the car and our soft
humming of song slivers to keep us awake.
There was that last night when Chalo squeezed
himself between us in the back seat. Somewhere
around Willowbrook he wanted to touch my breast,
and I let him. Yeah, we knew so much
back then, you and I. So much.

Blizzards to Go

I see Old Women
at the Dairy Queen counting
copper pennies for cones—
three here and six blizzards
to go.

Old Women holding to knobby canes
and each other in their intricate two step
waltz across the linoleum floor
to the red plastic booth,

Old Women talc-dry, blue hair
from Baldwin's Beauty School.....finger curled
across the top, bobby pinned in place,
black leatherette
purses—shiny clasped,

Old Women with sensible shoes,
doe shadowed eyes, and crimson lips
that once were kissed.

Redemption on the Drag

at Veggie Thyme

I passed him on my way in—a standing pile
of dirty rags—his long blond
dreadlocks matted with brown oak leaves

Through the window I tried not to watch
as his eyes scanned the paper menu,
tried not to notice as he counted the coins
in his hand

He came into the small table-stuffed room,
walked by me, I could have reached out
to touch this mother's son

I caught my breath as his smell filled the spring room,
seemed to cast its self against the green
rain forest wallpaper

"*Brown rice,*" he said to the venerable woman
behind the counter, "*just brown rice, to go,
and water, maybe some water, please.*"

As he turned to go, my savory lavender
rice, steamed in limp lotus leaves
turned to dust in my mouth.

Andy Kaufman

Late last night on the flickering screen
your face falsely pleaded for understanding.
"*I don't think you're laughing with me,*"
you said over and over in your pale little voice.
Even then the tumor pressed and waited
until the time was right, until you could take no more.
Did you know? As you danced your dance
beyond the third wall,
and your unblinking eyes stared wildly-wide.

In Lexa's Garden

At point the white cat, blaze
faced, picks one foot
up, touches lightly
the wet grass.
With tense tail
it waits.

The chipmunk
sits still, not
breathing.

III

I Wait for the Owl's Call

Wreathed in clouds
only the islands listened
when you first called;
I was not ready.
Surely, it was another's name
you whispered,
I thought,
so close in sound to mine.

Once many war canoes
were pulled stem-first onto the shore,
among the wet
dark rocks,
between the scattered
clam shells
reflected bone-white
against the black sands
of Kingcome.

Eighty thousand
strong were we.
Now, our tribe scatters like campfire embers
pulled aloft by the wind
to fade in flight.
The spirits
of the white world
cloud our eyes; until the sadness
runs so deep, it seems
to stretch back to stain
our ancient mysteries.

Many scenes are stored: star-fall,
a young buck walks through the village
chants, herring swelled straits
and the flash of eagle's claws,
snow laid thick on shoulders
of green-grey spruce and winter's chill.

They say, chiefs return sleek and black of body
like the raven; I am ready.
I have blown my breath into the dried kelp,
 now, my wife wears it loosely around her neck,
close to her heart.

There is a light burning through the trees
like ceremonial house fires
where the old ones kept their ways.
Someone waits in the night for my return, I wait
to hear your call.

In the novel I Heard the Owl Call My Name, *by Margaret Craven, an owl calls out the name of the next to die among the Tsawataincuk Tribe of Kingcome Village, BC.*

Dorothy Ellis Barnett

Circles of Power

From the bloody buffalo hump,
the tough skin was stripped
then laid to rest wet
in a hollow of the ground
until it was hard and shaped
like the bowl of my outstretched hand.

From the sky Spider Woman,
friend of Thunder, came to weave
a black trail for Eagle to follow;
his wind-shadow touched
one white shaft

against the braided sweetgrass.
We raised our voices to the enemy
with the shields' murmured blessings
whispering close to our ears.

The red shields the chiefs slung
carried such sweet dreamed medicine
that bullets ran like the tears
of our lost children.

Oaxaca

beside the road

In the winter heat of Monte Alban,
a sundark woman plunges

her hand into a washtub of ice
to fish out sweetly blemished oranges.

Her splayed feet puff dry
dust into the air.

She slices the pocked moons
onto the cracked tabletop;

the orange life drips into
a plastic bag.

The Thirties

for Dorothea Lang

My boxy instrument caught forever
the teetering despair of the Oklahoma dust bowl,
long-lonely California roads, and tent cities
where wheat farmers and cotton pickers, alike,
mixed into the veneer of liquid poverty spreading west.

In one a washerwoman in faded black and white silk stares
into the camera, forgotten child on her lap.
My shutter clicks to close the moment when
she remembers her grandmother's silver pin
abandoned deep in the empty pocket
of her husband's wool coat back home.

In another a man remembers happy sunlight
and following fat brown cows across green pastures
to evening milk and yellow grain.
He remembers a harvest when hawks circled overhead,
remembers when there was promise of more.

Think of the times when even the world seems to turn
against its self, seems to pound the sun into the thirsty earth,
what are we supposed to do, if not to save it for the future.

What Georgia O'Keefe Lost in Santa Fe, New Mexico

Words escaped her like the dust of dry bones
she raked into the lengthening shadows
of the Sangre Cristo Mountains.
She searched for them under the sagging feather bed;
she searched between the gray warp and red weft
of the Chief's blanket rug but her tongue could not find
them.

Word-threads she could recall were sticky in her mind:
knob became handle, stick became hammer, squash blossom
became old friend.
Soon she had nothing except colors and cactus brushes to
speak to the sky.
The brush said, "*Blue*." She layered her reply, "*White*," But it
didn't matter.
Ripe leaf-layers pushed out green from canvas
intruding, "*Lilac*" into the conversation.

She went on for days speaking desert hues to the clouds.
The sky advanced then retreated bruised blacks
around the opening peony blossoms. Dark rain clouds
caressed the pink tips and she forgot
not knowing. Across the valley a rusty iron bell clanged
and she remembered *white pesole*, she remembered *blue corn tortillas* warm from the fire,
she remembered *the bite of red chile* on her tongue.

Dorothy Ellis Barnett

Afternoon Roads

I dream afternoon roads
of golden hills, green pines
oaks dusty—where
does this road lead

I sing, a lonely traveler
on the road as evening falls
and it grows late

Once passion's thorn
pierced my heart, I pulled
it out—I cannot feel
my heart

All the countryside is quiet
in somber meditation
as the wind sounds
in the populars by the river

Still the darkness comes
the road winds and shows
a feeble white, growing dim
then disappearing, waiting for no one

My song returns to its moan,
"*oh, sharp, golden thorn*
would that my heart, again,
feel your stinging bite."

Translation: "Yo Voy Sonando Caminos" by Antonio Machado

Dreaming God

Last night as I lay sleeping
I dreamed a holy vision
A mystic fountain rose
from my depths—pure watery
spring I've never tasted

Last night as I lay sleeping
I dreamed a holy vision
Within my heart golden
bees made white
wax and sweet honey
from old bitterness

Last night as I lay sleeping
I dreamed a holy vision
A red glowing sun beamed
burning from my heart,
and I wept

Last night as I lay sleeping
I dreamed a holy vision
and my heart held God.

Translation: "*Anoche Cuando Dormia*" by Antonio Machado

Dorothy Ellis Barnett

IV

Amendment 25

Article 4

The orange faced man shouts, "*lock her up!*"
and the crowd chants: "*lock her up!.... lock her up!*"

The orange faced man swoops his flax colored hair
over his thin-skinned head and says,
"*Yes, folks, we are gonna do that. We're gonna do that.*"

The great halls of the white house are not gilded enough
for the orange faced man with swooping flax hair...he must
go down to the sea again, to the gilt...the golf...the sand.

At night he dreams of purpled domes in a foreign land;
the orange faced man wakes to fading power and
questions, never ending questions, but he has no
answers. He shouts, "*Fake news, fake news.*"

The orange faced man claims, "*wire tapping,*" but
doesn't mean it literary; he claims victory, but he is not
popular with most of the people. "*Find the leaks,
that's the real crime,*" he claims.

The orange faced man gathers his forces, circles
his children closer, ends his tweets with the word,
"*sad,*" as the real world closes in.

What will he shout when they come for him?

Flying into Baltimore

The plane breaks through the winter storm sky,
skims over lacy bare trees for miles.
Only scraps of foliage remain among the snow
dripped shades of gray, brown and black.
This land looks used up, below
nothing stirs.

Young men in the seats behind talk endlessly
about the journey of one – the coming war,
desert heat soon to consume him,
and making wills.

What do you do? Asks the one not going. *They
show me photos, the other answers; I tell them
where to bomb. We can hit a man's eye, if
we want to – I don't tell many folks.*

Nameless tributaries braid themselves into
the Chesapeake, then settle into shimmering, frozen
fingers of water as the soft voices speak
the unspeakable, the unthinkable.

Avoiding the storm above and
the ground below we fly under
the clouds like this for miles into Baltimore.

And it needs to be spring again and new green
needs to shoot up faster than the harvester
can cut it and the earth should be waiting for that
because there needs to be a time when there's not
talk of death and wills from young men
as they fly into Baltimore.

Dorothy Ellis Barnett

U.S. Invasion of Iraq—

With Respect to Langston Hughes

(Since May 1, 2003, when President Bush declared that major combat operations in Iraq had ended, 792 U.S. soldiers have died according to the Defense Department, A.P., Aug.14, 2004)

This is for the kids who die,
in the far-off places of Tikrit, Basra,
Baghdad, the Shiite holy city
of Najaf, away from green
mountains, lush trees of white
magnolia, or in their own simple
beds in stone-walled cities

Kids will die in the drowning red sand
and blowing winds across endless
miles in foreign heat as tanks and
Humvees rumble past while
men talk of religion or the politics
of rightness as women wear black
and children cry

*Of course the wise and the learned
who* speak as foreign journalists,
presidents, and generals declare
victory over Sadam as kids torture
kids in Abu Ghraib and martyred
bombers leave their calling cards
because they haven't heard yet
"*mission accomplished*"

Listen, kids who die-
you didn't do anything wrong
and maybe your bodies will come
home in the lonely blackness of
midnight un-noticed, or maybe you
will go unnoticed in the sand, maybe
you will be wrapped in clean cloth
before that first shovel of dirt hits your face,
or maybe your death song will float
you into the heavenly skies on lilting
Arabic notes, pounding Bruce
Springsteen, or rapping Tupac,

But listen, you didn't do anything
wrong, *kids who will die*, American,
European or Middle Eastern; this is not
your war far from home or next door,
remember you didn't do anything wrong
and the chicken hawks who let kids die,
will someday taste iron in their mouths, too.

Near and Far

Knowing little of trade centers and planes
a small brown lizard inches along—intent
on nothing more than a patch of warmth
on the weathered fence

A tailless Mediterranean gecko scurries down
the warm wall of the courtyard while thousands
of hands move twisted steel, DNA, and broken glass

The cardinal flies its bright red
into the birdfeeder—seeds spill and in dark
tunnels dust drifts down covering silent
counters of cards and gifts

Large white-winged doves cluster
on the pink sandstone, call out their soft lament
while somewhere light reaches through shadows
hands hold to hands,
voices call *hold on, hold on*

Schoolyard sounds float out into the street,
cars whiz past to run red lights,
and young zealots dream of martyrdom

We are told to go on, so I dig my hands into the dark earth
and plant purple fall asters, repot the pomegranate,
sweep the spilled dirt from the patio,

We are told to go on, so I touch my husband in the night,
embrace this moment
expect nothing more

We are told to go on, so I write this poem—these words

Now, what?

WASHINGTON—U.S. officials say the detailed surveillance photos and documents that prompted higher terror warnings dated from as far back as 2000 and 2001, and Homeland Security Secretary Tom Ridge said Tuesday the government concluded "it was essential" to publicize it and raise the terror alert. Yahoo News—Dated August 3, 2004

So they raise their terror
alert to orange – high
drama and we
are supposed to jump
at the sound of every click,
we are supposed to question
every shade of brown skin,
we are supposed to feel
secure by the concrete
barricading buildings,
we are supposed to go
on with our lives,
we are supposed to vigilantly
shop, and we the People of the
United States of America
are supposed to vote
for Bush the Protector.

Girl Protection

for India's daughters

I.
In the village there is the pensive calling
of birds in the dark green foliage
shadowed by distant mountains.

Oleanders white, fuchsia, light pink
flowers, beautiful swaying in summer's
heat, grandmothers know your dark
green leaves and straight spiked stems hide
the milky poison in your sap.

II.
It's a girl comes the unhappy cry,
and grandmothers gather in the yard,
cut bitter green stems to milk
while shadowed mothers refuse to nurse
their daughters.

Sons can light the swaying pyre so smoky
souls ascend to heaven,
but not girls who need dowries
of gold and rupees then move away.

III.
Did you find your voice too soon so
they split your tongue to silence
you
or

did you wave your baby arms
too high,
kick your legs too hard on the diapering
table so they had to break
your bones to still you,
or
maybe your vulva invited the intrusion,
the abuse.

Did they not have beautiful oleander waiting
in the side yard dark green shadowed
by distant mountains. Dark
green gathered by grandmothers'
hands, dripping sticky white sap.

IV.
Don't encourage her to find
her voice; she'll only want a life
and gold earrings; she'll want to move
out of the shadows.

Beautiful oleander, swaying pungent
scent offers a way out
as shadowed grandmothers gather
in the village and mourners cover the dead
with white, fuchsia, light pink
flowers. Flaming pyres float on swirling water,
carry the burning beautiful
oleander to distant mountains.

"I touched their feet"

Pakistan–gang-rape punishment–Friday, July 5, 2002—AP

There is sadness seeping in the black
and white photo I carried with me for weeks;
sadness folded into a tiny square. Sadness
secure in my pocket through New Mexico,
Colorado; I carried it past the billboards of
polygamy in Utah into the green forests of Oregon
and Puget Sound.

In the photo white burka swathes
the young woman, white purity
in our culture, far from that
in hers. Raped by her tribe's men
for a walk unchaperoned,
a walk not by her, but by her brother.

Tribal justice, punishment, gang-rape, shame,
her mother wails in the background as the young
woman moans to those who would listen, "*I touched
their feet, but they tore my clothes and raped me
one by one.*"

Once long ago, I let an older cousin kiss me
at night under summer stars when I was eleven;
what would this tribal council have done to me
because of him?

Canton, Texas

c. Fall, 1993

*"We have quite a
few here.
You'll see'm—down
past Tyler Street.
They've got their own
section. Keep their
yards real
nice—and every
thing.*

*They don't bother
us none—never did,
but*

*you know, can't find
a one of 'em these
days that wants to
clean—or work over to
the nursin'
home.*

*And use to be
they'd line up
for miles to work
over at Grand Saline."*

Sometime Sweetness

Racism is hidden on the bottom shelf—
dark curtained—collecting dusty motes—
sometimes when I reach past to a higher
level, searching for that sometimes
sweetness, I accidentally touch against it—
brushing loose the fragile, honey thick
pieces—they settle softly, heavy around
my feet.

Escarpment

Past Henly, half-way to Blanco
the winding road rises to meet the sky,
stocktanks and scrub cedars
stretch below in limitless landscape,

A red-winged hawk floats in spirals
down, then up, then down,
the earth, the world itself
is caught in this moment
where season has no meaning

Against the cliffs, rosy star-flowers
clutch to crumbling limestone
in this mid-summer heat,
a mere handful of mountain pinks
their roots pulling water from air

I, too, am rooted here, try to forget
that croplands and pastures
sprout into suburbs and
black-top drifts into white
concrete and dividers, try to forget
this land has been here forever

Cedar Fever

Some trees have trunks straight as sticks
and the bark peels off in long smooth pieces
exposing the white-lady skin underneath.

Some trees have trunks of knotted twists,
crooked as hands that hold flood gates shut,
and the bark is bumpy-scarred like a leper's face.

The tree outside my window has a trunk
neither crooked nor straight, but rilled its length,
and its bark peels off in long stringy strips that smell of cedar.

The tree outside my window wears
on its green a dusting of orange
powder that puffs up in the wind
as if the wild woods have taken to fire.

Spring

The cedar waxwings came today—settled heavy
in the bare boughs of the Arizona ash
wintering in the side yard. The slender branches bowed
low under the grey weight of so many feathers.

Each year they come, take over the landscape,
eat the ripening mulberries—white and
amethyst droppings everywhere.

Silvered flashes of red, yellow smother out
the persistent jays and mockingbirds;
all that energy—like the determined ring of the phone
and your voice on the other side.

Broom-star

On the chalky road
they stood still, heads tilted
back, and there
past the dark outline of the scrub
cedar, past the black fringed collar
cast by the oak,
the shutter opened and
stayed what their eyes
recorded into the back recesses
where there stirred a whisper

like breath through silk,
some memory-vague,
of high plains,
of rounded head on one horizon
and fading tail stretched
clear across to the other
like a giant celestial smear in the dark.

As if, in this almost-memory,
there had been darkness unmeasurable
brighten before by this blaze.

As if, in tall grass, bison had stopped their sleep
to lift brown woolly heads night after night
towards the returning nebula,
and mosquitoes stilled their endless
drone to listen.

As if, before when there was no naming,
in all the nests and burrows, on all the trails
when no one had yet stepped onto the tundra,
the wolf and badger, coyote and quail, lizard
and bird,

as if, something in all their memories stirred too,
about that first time
imagine what a sight that must have made
when there was no one to tell it.

Enchanted Rock

I.
After the ritual tequila,
salt, lime, after the burn
hits low, we cross
the dry creek bed

to walk in the night.
Tide-like the winds crash
over the grass
into the banked trees,
crest, froth at peak,

recede to reform the swell.
Its whisper our siren's call
faint in the distance

then roaring around us
where we stand by the wintering oak,
dig ourselves into the hillside,
hold fast to the limestone.

II.
On the top where the last of the rain
is held by small pools, I spread my sleeping bag,
to watch stars when the sky is black as nothing,
and the moon has yet to rise.

One by one like pin pricks
through inky cloth, they light
where only moments before
just liquid dark spread out.

There, where a three-pronged prickly pear
holds to granite fast, the ring-tailed raccoon
comes to wash its night-find.

III.
Thigh-high grass dry as tinder
moves out of our way
when we pass into the night.
The near gibbous moon
shadows the Spanish oak and sumac,
washes out the flame to black

and the domed pink granite
reflects like snow.
As we pass the spiked-sotol

only the chilling wind listens
and moves with us
onto the plane.

Out among the tasajillo
and the prickly pear-thorns sharp
as snake bite, we move
like night travelers,

two ruts—our path
the emerging stars—our guides
the moon—our breath.

Wild Things

Our back yard is a wild tangle of trees left
to birds, 'possums and robber baron raccoons.

One April morning when the noisy cedar waxwings bathed
in the fountain by our front door, a fat 'possum
waddle past their gray comings and goings.

She must have been pregnant, her round belly almost touching
the pink sandstone patio; her passengers waiting for that
    moment of light.
I thought of her and her mate love-embracing somewhere in
    the woods.

Some might believe their coupling guided by a cosmic
    yearning,
where the stars aligned just right, but perhaps his nearsighted
    eyes
preferred the soft darkness of no moon with only desire to
    steer the way.

I can imagine her scent wafting in the air, he following,
nose up, captivated by her pungent ripeness,
she leading him on, unaware of his approach, her pink nose
    to the ground.

Did she swoon at his touch or did she feign disinterest,
coyly choosing instead to nibble at a plump white grub.
Did they lie on a soft bed of leaves layered with musky smells.
Did the heavens move for them when at last they found each
    other.

Bly's Dust

Finding Texas

on the way to Round Top

There is remembered loneliness in the sprawling
oaks sheltering the crumbling well-houses.
Blue bonnets and barbed wire lean against fence posts.
The car hums as Warrenton and Winedale float by lost to
time.

Fields of pink phlox and orange-red paintbrush push
over rolling hills. The city mantle slips
away as a sprinkling of cows amble to breakfast
while across the road clucking
white chickens scratch in a gravel yard.

Ahead someone turns onto a long dirt drive,
in the distance a fading farmhouse waits.
Imagine their life where the moon rises
over quiet and the neighbor's lights are always on.

Imagine marrying Henry who lived out by Noonday.
Twenty years older when he came courting,
there could have been six or seven kids with him
and plastic red roses in a milk-white vase
on top of the television.

There could have been nothing else but a blacktop road
where a gray misty haze settles on ponds
and spring green gardens.

Dorothy Ellis Barnett

The Necessity of Empty Places

Autumn, Central Texas

When I woke to clear stillness
of black-straight up, close

to the gibbous moon, a white wisp
of v stretched swiftly south.

My blanket held frost
like a field of blue diamonds.

Twice the lead changed,
curling smoke. Only

a distant honking
broke the night.

"The question is not what you look at, but what you see."
— *Henry David Thoreau*
Journal of 5 August, 1851

V
Ansel Adams– Yosemite Photography

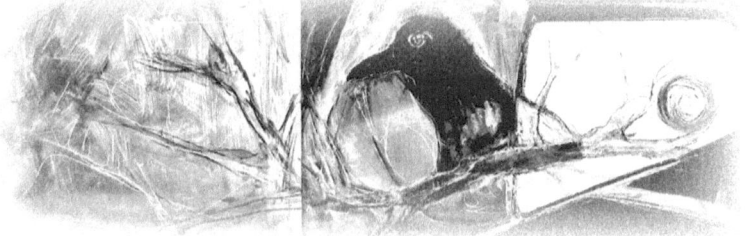

Spring/Water

Petaled rain falls against
the creek like torn lace,

rushes down to swim
in eddies between the rocks.
My shutter opens — white

froth freezes in shallow rapids
reaching for black trunks.

A response to: *Tenaya Creek, Dogwood, Rain, Yosemite National Park, California, c. 1948*

Winter/Water

*"Sit from morning till night under some willow bush
on the river bank where there is a wide view,"*
— John Muir

or go down by the snow hummocks in winter

    when the day's sun has sculpted the snowed

rocks into puffs of white,

    and the nameless

water that skates around the low hills

slides

    into Tenaya Lake.

A response to: *Snow Hummocks, Yosemite National Park, California, c. 1949*

Winter/Air

We haven't seen
another 'cept kin
for months,   caught
here, between valleys,

peaks deep enough to keep
ground-shadows 'till midday.

There's been no other female
voice to reach my ears
        since Kansas.
Once down by the river
I saw the Indian woman wading through,
but wind-quick she melted
among the pines.

Snow's banked up and over
the tallest side of the cabin.
Warmth comes rarely
        and never to my feet.

A response to: *North Dome, Royal Arches, Washington Column, Winter, Yosemite National Park, California, c. 1940*

Summer/Water

My piano suffered; its rival the cadence
of water on gray granite rock, the murmur
against feathered mossy banks. My family
and friends said don't loose the music.

Little did they know what choirs I found
in water seeking the next level, down
down, the succession of chords sounding
above all else, down to the pianissimo found
whispering on the valley floor

A response to: *Yosemite Falls and Point, Yosemite Valley c. 1936*

Dorothy Ellis Barnett

Spring/Air

I wish I could tell momma,
about this place, this high meadow,
stretching out past tall-green timber
to the distant clouded mountains
just now waking from winter.

I wish I could tell momma,
that little Carl died a while back,
that his poor pale body just seemed
to give out with all the coughing. That's three
babies gone now.

I wish I could tell momma,
about the color that comes
with spring – blues, reds, all kinds
of yellows, and a purple-veil hazing
everything at evening.

I wish I could tell momma, that we
gave him a proper service when
the ground thawed, his small body
wrapped in a piece of cloth I'd been saving
for Oregon and I read from the scriptures,
in the valley of the shadow of death....

A response to: *Mount Gibbs, Dana Fork, Upper Tuolumne Meadows, Yosemite National Park c. 1946*

Spring/Earth

Past the sunlight, the woman washes
herself in shallow water now spring-warm.
Her pale skin shines wet so different
from mine.

Fire knows the way to the nut
buried deep in cone – life force
to the tree. Ground between hard
rocks – stone against stone – it will
sweeten my mouth.

She knows the way to the berries deep
in the woods and where eggs can be
found. I have left eagle's feather
for her child.

A response to: *Forest Floor, Yosmite Valley c. 1950*

Summer/Earth

Even a fallen tree has beauty
in the raw, naked way it stretches
into the lake, back to source.

Even these bare branches grace
the frame reaching as they do
for the sky.

And the lake holds the image
far longer than my camera: the clouds,
thick grass, the gentle cradle
the sleeping water makes day after day.

A response to: *Siesta Lake, Yosemite National Park, California, c. 1958*

Fall/Air

Along the bank of this nameless lake,
tall and twisted – the pines pirouette
up to watch mirrored
in the stillness
the frozen grass-dance.

My sleepy body molded
its self to gathered branches
and there was only clear stillness
of black- close to the gibbous moon.

Frost spread out like a blanket wet with
blue diamonds, only a distant honking
broke the night.

A response to: *Lodgepole Pines, Lyell Fork of the Merced River, Yosemite National Park, c. 1921*

Fall/Earth

I do not want to forget the direction
of the moon's rise on a clear night –
that way's east towards home, east
where miles of desolation runs
to Kansas.

The full moon rose last night
while I lay dreaming of the sod house
and howling, windy plains
where yesterday's past
was left behind.

I do not want to forget what
I thought to carry with me: my sister's
voice singing with the pump organ,
hauling water for miles during
droughts, dust every where.

We were cut down into that flat prairie,
had to be to weather the storms. It's not
much better here. I do not want to forget
my sister's voice singing with the pump
organ we couldn't carry.

A response to: *Moon and Half Dome, Yosemite Valley,* c. *1960*

Summer/Air

Far below, I have seen the woman,
and, over the sound of the wind,
heard her cough.

In a valley away from the elk,
she lives as an animal
in a den of sticks

with no way for fire-smoke
to leave. Her breath
will go soon. I will stand

here to sing her leaving
to the farthest peaks, and hope
her husband stands by the falls

to catch my song. I will watch
her pass with the shadows
across the mountains.

A response to: *High Sierra from Washburn Point, Yosemite National Park, California, c.1935*

Dorothy Ellis Barnett

Winter/Earth

Wet snow coats black branches
thick as cotton batting where
the woods go on and on,
so thick depth is questionable.

The obedient eye captures
what it wants: sacred groves, grottos
of forest floor, light and dark
every where – benediction evident.

It is here in this small opening
between black and white, where
I am most alone listening,
seeing. It is here in this soft gray
where I am most at home.

A response to: *Cedar Trees, Winter, Yosemite Valley c. 1949*

Gratitude

I'VE ALWAYS BELIEVED that we come into this world alone and gather/attract our family along our life's journey. I have been so fortunate to meet the following people who have loved me and walked with me and supported me and mentored me, so that there is this writing. From the University of Texas: Kurth Sprague, Jim Magnuson, Naomi Shihib Nye, David Wevill, and Pattiann Rogers—I am so grateful that you didn't close doors, quite the opposite, you showed me what was possible and valued what I had to say. From Pacific Lutheran University I thank: Judith Kitchen, Stan Rubin, and Peggy Shumaker. I give thanks also to Wendy Barker and Judith Barrington for wonderful workshops and patient teaching. I am indebted to friends who have encouraged me and put up with me, and the rare good luck we found each other.

For giving my writing a home, I am grateful to Alamo Bay Press and Pam Booton for understanding the creative process. For brilliant insights and careful work with the text and layout, I am especially indebted to Terry Sherrell and George Anne Chalmers at OneTouchPoint-Southwest Printing.

Of course, there is always my love and gratitude for my husband and daughters, and son-in-law, and my grandchildren who still walk with me.

About Dorothy Ellis Barnett

DOROTHY ELLIS BARNETT landed in Austin, Texas after a hardscrabble childhood growing up on the riverbeds, campgrounds and roads of the Southwest. While at The University of Texas she obtained a B.A. in Anthropology, an M.A. in English and was awarded a James A. Michener Fellowship. Together with her Fellows, she founded Borderlands: Texas Poetry Review, then went on to launch The Rio Review and Poetry at Round Top leaving over 50 literary journals in print along the literary highway. These publications have promoted, encouraged, and inspired countless writers and artists.

Dorothy subsequently earned her M.F.A. from Pacific Lutheran University. She is now Professor Emerita at Austin Community College where she founded and created the Creative Writing Department. She is a former Board Member of the Writers' League of Texas and is currently on the organizational committee for Poetry at Round Top held at Festival Hill each Spring. While her path has left a legacy for the literary community that includes her own publications, it pales in comparison to her role as wife, mother, grandmother and friend.

About the Cover Artist

REJINA (REJI) THOMAS lives and works in Austin, Texas. Her acclaimed artwork is held in public places and private collections around the world. Ms. Thomas has supported the arts for decades by generously sharing her studio, Pine Street Station with the Austin arts community. Pine Street Station was one of the original participants in the East Austin Studio Tour. Most recently, her work was featured in an historic solo show at the George Carver Museum in Austin. Her paintings are beautiful, bold, big and colorful. She says that the work serves as a reminder of the tragic pasts that are ever evolving and are connected by enduring primitive symbols and spiritual ascension. Visit Reji at www.rejithomasart.com

Also by Dorothy Ellis Barnett

Road Songs: A Memoir

The Almost Stories
The Memory Comes of Water – Chapbook
The Necessity of Empty Places – Chapbook

www.ingramcontent.com/pod-product-compliance
Lightning Source LLC
Chambersburg PA
CBHW030120100526
44591CB00009B/474